FACE TO FACE WITH
POLAR BEARS

by Norbert Rosing
with Elizabeth Carney

NATIONAL GEOGRAPHIC

WASHINGTON, D.C.

FACE TO FACE

◀ *A slumbering giant: Polar bears are one of the largest land carnivores in the world.*

One fall, my wife Elli and I had a single goal: to photograph polar bears. We were staying at a research camp outside "the polar bear capital of the world"—the town of Churchill in Manitoba, Canada.

Taking pictures of polar bears is amazing but also dangerous. Polar bears—like all wild animals—should be photographed from a safe distance. When I'm face to face with a polar bear, I like it to be through a camera with a telephoto lens. But sometimes, that is easier said than done. This was one of those times.

HOW BIG IS THIS BEAR?

- Polar bears are one of the largest land predators in the whole world.
- Paws can be 12 inches (30 cm) across—that's some foot!
- Males may weigh as much as a small car—over 1,700 pounds (770 kg).
- Male bears are as long as normal room height from floor to ceiling.

As Elli and I cooked dinner, a young male polar bear who was playing in a nearby lake sniffed, and smelled our spaghetti and garlic bread.

The hungry bear followed his nose to our camp, which was surrounded by a high, wire fence. He clawed, bit, and shoved the wire mesh. He stood on his hind legs and pushed at the wooden fence posts.

Terrified, Elli and I tried all the bear defense actions we knew. We yelled at the bear, banged pots, and fired blank shotgun shells into the air. Sometimes loud noises like these will scare bears off. Not this polar bear—he just growled and went back to trying to tear down the fence with his massive paws.

I radioed the camp manager for help. He told me a helicopter was on its way, but it would be 30 minutes before it arrived. Making the best of this close encounter, I snapped some pictures of the bear.

Elli and I feared the fence wouldn't last through 30 more minutes of the bear's punishment. The camp manager suggested I use pepper spray. The spray burns the bears' eyes, but doesn't hurt them.

So I crept up to our uninvited guest and, through the fence, sprayed him in the face. With an angry roar, the bear ran back to the lake to wash his eyes.

This young male polar bear tries to push down the fence that circles the camp. He was probably extra hungry because of a toothache, which made it difficult for him to chew. He was hoping for my spaghetti!

A few minutes later, the helicopter arrived. As we were lifted into the air, we saw the stubborn bear was already heading back to our camp.

When Elli and I got home and developed our pictures, we noticed this bear had broken an important tooth. Like humans, polar bears feel pain, have emotions, and can be afraid. Elli and I learned our lesson: Beware of a bear with a toothache.

MEET

A mother polar bear sits with her two cubs in Manitoba, Canada. Polar bears most commonly give birth to twins.

THE POLAR BEAR

Like a dog after a bath, a polar bear shakes water from its coat after a swim.

I started traveling to the Arctic to photograph wildlife 17 years ago. At first, I planned to photograph things like wildflowers and the northern lights. But my plans changed. I became fascinated with polar bears. The first time I looked into the eyes of a polar bear, I felt an important moment of connection. I knew this was the animal I was destined to capture on film for all to see. Since then, I have had my truck's tires slashed by a polar bear. I nearly lost my fingertips to frostbite. And I narrowly escaped becoming a bear's lunch after my truck got stuck in a snowdrift. Still, nothing has ruined my feeling of connection to this amazing animal.

Polar bears might look similar to their cousins, the land-dwelling black bears and brown bears. But besides their color, these white bears are different in one big way. Polar bears are marine mammals. Like seals and walruses, they spend most of their lives on the ocean. In fact, their scientific name, *Ursus maritimus,* means "sea bear."

The icy Arctic Ocean and lands that surround the North Pole are a polar bear's idea of paradise. These bears are built to keep warm in freezing temperatures. For much of the year, they spend their days sleeping in snowdrifts and playing, and hunting on sea ice.

Polar bears eat mainly the fat and meat of other animals. Seals are their favorite meals. They sometimes eat walruses and caribou, too. I've watched polar bears nab their prey in many different ways. In one common method, the bear stands very still

➡ *A bear feasts on one of its favorite meals, a walrus, in Igloolik, Canada. Polar* *bears don't bury leftovers for later meals the way other bears do.*

Polar bear range
On land   On pack ice

Polar bear denning sites

Maximum extent of winter pack ice

Country boundary

• Rare polar bear sightings

Polar bears live in the Arctic, near the North Pole. They are one of eight species of bears in the world. The only continents with no native bears are Australia, Antarctica, and Africa.

over a hole in the ice. Seals swim under the sea ice, but they must come to the surface to breathe. When a seal pops up for air, the bear grabs it.

After a meal, polar bears wash up. For polar bears, keeping clean is not just about looking good. A clean coat keeps bears warmer than a dirty one. Why? Polar bear hair looks white to us because it adopts the color of the light that hits it. Actually, it is colorless and hollow like a tube. It draws heat from sunlight to the bear's black skin below. This special coat also helps the bears blend into the snowy landscape.

Adult bears have perfected the art of keeping warm. Polar bear cubs need help from their moms to keep from freezing to death.

To prepare for her cubs' birth, a soon-to-be mother bear digs a den. Dens are usually caves dug into earth or snow. They have long, narrow entrance tunnels to keep the mother's warmth from escaping outside. One scientist found a cozy den to be 37 degrees F (20 degrees C) warmer than the outside air.

The mother bear rests in the den for three to four months until cubs are born in the winter. Newborns have thin hair and no teeth. They are the size of a squirrel and depend on their mother for warmth, food, and shelter. They nurse on her fatty milk. The new family stays in the den until early spring, when the cubs are strong enough to journey to the sea ice.

↑ This polar bear cub rests on top of its mother's head. Mom doesn't seem to mind. Cubs stay with their mothers for up to two and a half years. She teaches them how to survive in their frosty world.

A POLAR PLACE

Imagine a place where wide stretches of ice go on for as far as the eye can see. In the winter, darkness lasts 24 hours a day. In the summer, the sun never sets at all, giving the place the nickname Land of the Midnight Sun. This is what the polar bears' home—the Arctic—is like.

The Arctic region lies north of the Arctic Circle— a line about three-fourths of the way up the globe from the equator. Inside the circle you'll find the Arctic Ocean, with the North Pole in the center

A polar bear shields his face from a blinding snowstorm.

15

↑ Mountain aven grows over rocks at Wapusk National Park. During the summer, wildflowers bloom and berries provide food for hungry polar bears.

HOW TO STAY WARM IN THE ARCTIC

- Three layers of socks
- Waterproof boots
- Three layers of pants
- Two turtlenecks
- Five layers of jackets
- Gloves, face mask, and hood
- Parka

and the northern-most lands of Russia, the United States (Alaska), Canada, Norway, and Denmark (Greenland).

Most of the time, a 6- to 8-foot-thick (1.8- to 2.4-meter) layer of ice covers the Arctic Ocean, which makes it the only ocean people and animals can walk on. Fish, seals, whales, and walruses swim below.

The Arctic isn't where you would want to spend a beach vacation. Below-freezing temperatures and stiff winds are the norm. There are few roads, so when I'm looking for polar bears, I use helicopters, snowmobiles, or dogsleds to get around.

While the land might seem harsh, it is really full of life. In the summer, wildflowers bloom in dazzling colors. You can find beetles, bees, and butterflies fluttering around. Almost 200 different types of birds—from puffins to snow geese—spend the warmer months breeding and nesting here.

What's the secret to surviving the Arctic's cold seasons? Keeping warm. For me, it's not easy. I wear many layers of clothes, a mask, hood, gloves, and waterproof boots. My equipment can also break in the Arctic's freezing temperatures. Sometimes my film gets so cold it shatters like glass in my hands.

← *A polar bear wanders a rocky coast in Canada while gulls look on. More than 175 types of birds migrate to the Arctic to breed in the summer.*

↓ *Polar bears are serious swimmers—they can swim distances of more than 100 miles. This mother and cub paddle through the freezing waters of Wager Bay.*

A harp seal pup lies on the ice. Polar bears most commonly eat ringed seals, bearded seals, and harp seals. Polar bears can sniff out a seal hiding under three feet (a meter) of ice from a mile (a kilometer and a half) away!

Young male bears play-fight. The bears are practicing for adulthood, when fights over females will be real and the stakes high.

Polar bears do a much better job of staying warm than humans. They have a big advantage: a built-in snowsuit. In addition to their special heat-absorbing coat and skin, bears have a 4-inch (10-centimeter) layer of fat called blubber. The blubber holds in the bears' body heat and also helps them float in water.

Polar bears have extra-wide paws that work like snowshoes. The paws spread out the bears' weight so they can balance on slippery ice and snow.

Polar bears are designed for Arctic survival. But even so, life in the Arctic isn't easy. These smart bears experiment with different ways to hunt, learn to avoid hunters, and perfect their den-making skills.

When two polar bears meet, anything can happen. I've been entertained for hours by watching young bears play-fight and wrestle. Older bears may fight over food or mates. Their heavily scarred faces are evidence of many battles. Mother bears protect their cubs at all costs from male polar bears and wolves.

Even though their lives in the Arctic are full of challenges, polar bears wouldn't be able to survive anywhere warmer. These bears live up to their nickname—Lords of the Arctic.

ON THIN ICE

Fortunately for polar bears, the Arctic is one area of the world where very few people live. Polar bears have avoided habitat destruction and overhunting, human activities that have landed other bears on the endangered species list.

But polar bears have other problems. Because of a worldwide warm-up, the Arctic ice is melting. In the past 50 years, average Arctic temperatures have increased by more than 5 degrees F (2 degrees C). This may not sound like much, but the heat is

⬆ *Workers from Manitoba Conservation—affectionately known as the polar bear police—relocate bears who get too close to people.*

enough to melt the sea ice earlier in the summer and cause it to freeze later in the fall. This shortens the bears' hunting time on the ice. Without enough time to hunt, eat, and build up fat, the bears may return to land weak and thin—and in danger of starving.

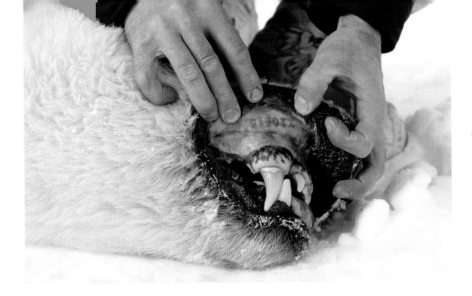

A scientist shows a bear's tattooed upper lip. Scientists tattoo bears, each with its own unique number, so the animals can be identified later.

Scientists hope to learn how polar bears are coping with their changing environment. How do you study a 1,700–pound (770–kilogram) bear? Very, very carefully. Scientists put the bear to sleep by shooting it with a drug-filled dart. Then they weigh the bear, take blood samples, and give it a checkup. The scientists fix numbered white tags to the bear's ears so it can be tracked and identified later. They also tattoo the bear's number to the inside of its upper lip.

In the past few years, researchers tracking polar bears have found dead bears floating in the water 60 miles (100 kilometers) off the coast of Alaska. The ice melted so quickly that these bears were stranded in the open ocean. They either died from exhaustion or drowned in rough waves and high winds.

Some Inuit hunters have told me that they have noticed changes in weather patterns and currents in

HOW TO HUNT LIKE A POLAR BEAR

- Hover above seal breathing holes and pounce when a seal appears

- Break the ice to get at young seals below

- Paddle through water toward seals resting on ice, with only your nose and eyes showing

- Follow your nose to find a dead whale, walrus, or caribou

- Watch out for melting sea ice

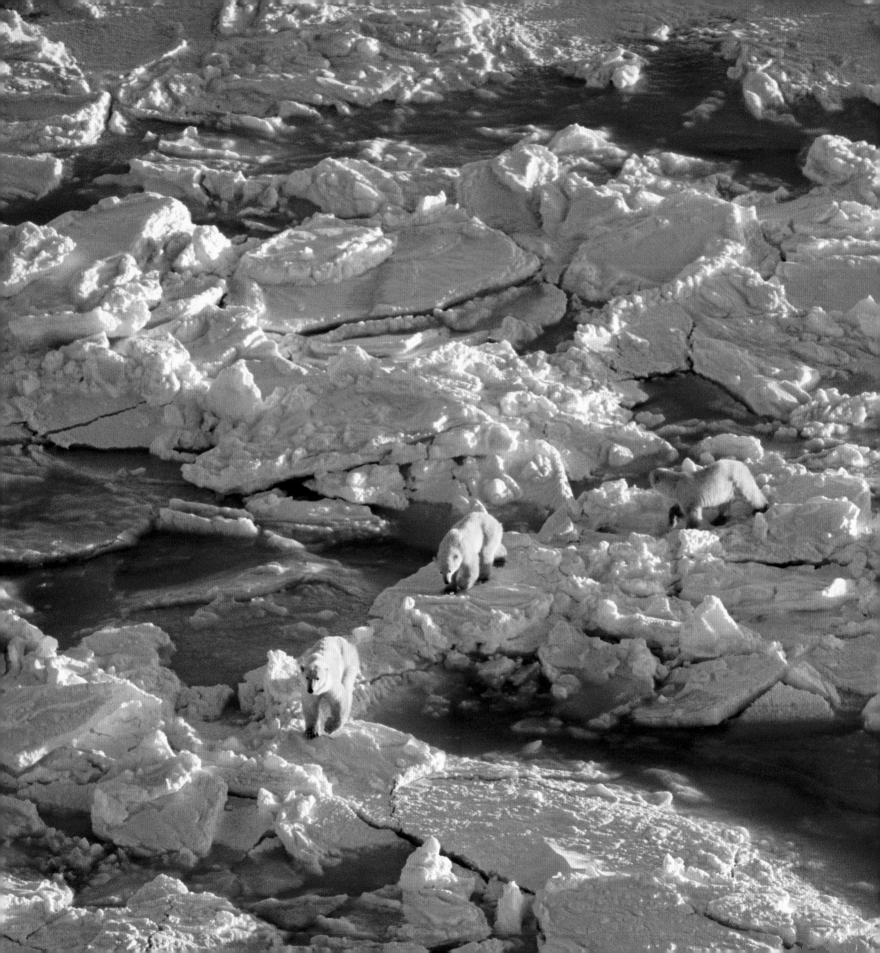

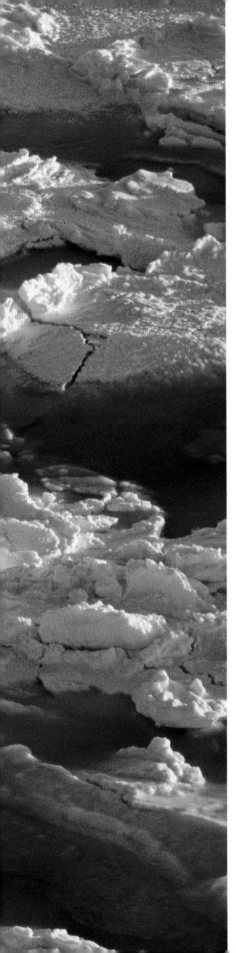

the region. These native Arctic people say that sometimes their feet even sink into melting permafrost (soil that's supposed to remain frozen year-round).

Most scientists believe the recent Arctic meltdown is part of a pattern called global warming. Global warming has been linked to the burning of fossil fuels, which power people's cars, planes, and factories. The burned fuels send gases, including carbon dioxide, into the air. When carbon dioxide builds up in the atmosphere, it can trap heat and warm the planet.

Right now, the world's some 25,000 polar bears are not endangered. But this can change. One study found that in 100 years, the Arctic will likely become 7 to 13 degrees F (4 to 7 degrees C) warmer. If this happens, the future of the polar bear and its home will be grim. But it's not too late to take action *(find out how on the next page).* It's my deepest hope that polar bears live to capture our imaginations forever.

HOW YOU CAN HELP

⬆ *Bears can't sign petitions. They need our help to keep their home protected.*

Global warming is the biggest threat polar bears face. If too much Arctic ice melts, their habitat will be destroyed. When we burn fuel to make electricity and to heat and cool homes, we add more carbon to the air. Carbon and gases in the air speed up global warming.

▬ You can help to slow this process. Try to use less power at home. Turn off the light when you leave a room. Turn off the TV unless you are really watching. If your home does not leak air, you will use less heating and cooling power. Ask your parents to check for tight windows, doors, and good insulation in the walls to prevent air leaks.

▬ Some electricity, called "green electricity," comes from wind and solar power. This type of energy does not add to global warming. Your family may be able to buy "green" through your local electric company. Ask your parents to find out about special programs like this.

▬ Gas engines in vehicles add carbon, too. Walk or ride a bike to get around, if you can do it safely. Could your family travel on public buses or trains for longer trips, instead of going by car?

▬ You can also help to protect polar bears by writing to your senators and representatives in Congress. Tell them you are worried about global warming. Ask them to make strict rules for car manufacturers and to favor cars with better gas mileage, hybrid engines, and all-electric cars. Ask them to support clean energy development and good bus and train systems.

▬ Learn all you can about polar bears and their environment. *(See the list of books and Web sites in Find Out More on page 30.)* Some animal welfare groups have special programs for young members. Joining a group that studies and works to preserve polar wildlife can be a big help to all the animals.

IT'S YOUR TURN

↓ *Making a snow angel or taking a bath? A polar bear rolls in the snow to clean its fur or maybe just to play.*

You might find captive bears in a nearby zoo. How will what you know about bears' habits help you get good pictures? Bears do many different things during the day. What would you most like to see them doing? Swimming? Eating? Playing? When do you think is the best time to see each of these activities? How do you think captive bear behavior differs from wild bear behavior? How is a bear's zoo environment different from its natural habitat? You can record your thoughts in a journal and then compare them later against your observations.

1 Imagine you could study wild polar bears. What behavior interests you the most? What else is there to learn about polar bears?

2 What would you need to take with you, besides your camera? What else would help you work in comfort in the Arctic? Would you need special clothes? How long would you stay? Would you need shelter? What kind?

3 You have read that polar bears roam over hundreds of miles during the year. Where would you go to see them hunting seals? What time of year would you see this?

4 Some wildlife protection groups take kids north to see Arctic animals, including polar bears. Maybe you can go on such a trip—and take your camera along!

FACTS AT A GLANCE

↑ *A cub chews on a twig. Polar bear cubs are playful and curious. They can turn almost any object into a toy.*

Scientific name
Ursus maritimus

Common names
Polar bear, ice bear, sea bear

Population
Between 20,000 and 27,000 worldwide. The International Union for Conservation of Nature and Natural Resources (IUCN) lists the polar bear as a "vulnerable" species. That means that wild polar bears are at risk of dying out.

Size
Polar bears are the largest species of bear (by record).

Length
Males up to 8'6" (2.6 m)
Females up to 6'11" (2.1 m)

Weight
Males up to 1,800 lbs. (800 kg)
Females up to 660 lbs. (300 kg)

Lifespan
Wild bears live 15-18 years. Zoo bears may live longer. The oldest captive polar bear known lived to be more than 40 years old.

Color
Polar bear skin is black. You can see the skin at the tip of their noses and on the pads of their feet. Polar bear coats look white, cream-colored, or yellowish, depending on the light, but each hair is colorless and hollow.

Special features
Polar bear bodies are well built to help them live in the Arctic. Their small ears do not lose much heat. The soles of their feet are mostly covered in fur, to keep them warm walking over ice. They grow a thick layer of fat under their skin that blocks the cold. To help them swim, polar bears have webbed toes on their forepaws. Polar bears don't hibernate like other bears.

Habitat
Polar bears spend much of the year on sea ice in the Arctic Ocean. A bear may travel across more than a thousand miles (over 1,500 kilometers) on the ice each year. They also roam coastal areas and islands, including parts of the United

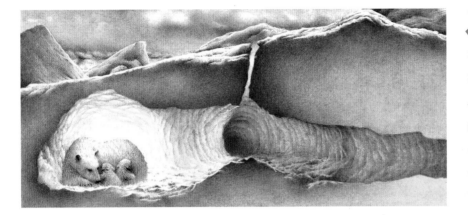

Pregnant females stay in their den from mid-October to as late as mid-April. During that time, mothers give birth to cubs and nurse them until they're big enough to survive the harsh weather outside the den.

States, Canada, Russia, Norway, and Greenland. A bear that lives in one place may roam over 200 square miles (500 square kilometers) of personal territory.

Food

Ringed seals are the main food polar bears hunt year-round. They also eat bearded seals, walruses, and beached whales. The blubber (fat layer) is the part of their prey they like best. Near towns and at human campsites, bears look through garbage dumps for food. Like other bear species, hungry polar bears will eat almost anything they can find.

Reproduction

Bears mate in the spring. Males and females do not stay together. The females find or dig a den in the earth or in deep, hardened ice. From one to three cubs are born there the following winter. Mother bears give birth and raise the cubs alone. Cubs stay with their mother until they are about 2½ years old.

Social habits

Adult polar bears usually live alone. At mating time, two or three male bears may follow one female. Mothers travel with cubs until the cubs are almost as big as adults. Cubs from the same litter may live together awhile after they leave their mother. Several bears may share the meat when a whale carcass washes up on shore. Bears living near Hudson Bay in Canada are often seen in groups as they look for food scraps left by humans.

Biggest threats

The worst threat to polar bears is loss of habitat through global warming and Arctic development. Bears cannot get enough food when their hunting areas of sea ice grow smaller. Chemical pollution on Arctic lands and in the water poisons bears. Chemicals get into most Arctic animals, including animals that polar bears eat. Polar bears in polluted areas are smaller and weaker. Fewer cubs are born where pollution is high.

GLOSSARY

Carnivore: an animal whose diet is based on meat.

Environment: the natural surroundings, including terrain, climate, and other native living things, of a plant or animal.

Fossil fuel: coal, oil, and natural gas. These fuels come from the slow breakdown of ancient plants or animal bodies over millions of years.

Global warming: a gradual rise in average temperatures worldwide.

Habitat: the place where a plant or an animal naturally lives.

Inuit: native peoples in the Arctic areas of Alaska, Siberia, Canada, and Greenland.

Marine: living in or near the sea or ocean, or depending on the ocean's food sources.

Norm: a usual state or condition.

North Pole: a point at the northern end of the Earth's axis, located in the Arctic Ocean. There, six months of daylight are followed by six months of darkness each year.

Permafrost: ground, soil, or rock that stays at a temperature of 32 degrees Fahrenheit (0°C) or below for two years or more.

Species: a group of animals or plants that look similar, breed with each other, and whose offspring can also breed successfully.

Telephoto lens: a camera lens that can act like a telescope, making distant objects appear close.

Tundra buggy: a special-purpose vehicle like a bus, used for observing Arctic wildlife safely. Buggies ride high on big tires over ice and snow instead of roads.

FIND OUT MORE

Books & Articles

Biel, Timothy Levi. Zoobooks 2. *Polar Bears.* Poway, CA: Wildlife Education, 1985.

Mangelson, Thomas D., and Bruemmer, Fred. *Polar Dance: Born of the North Wind.* Omaha, NE: Images of Nature, 1997.

National Audubon Society. *Guide to Marine Mammals of the World.* New York: Alfred A Knopf, 2002.

Patent, Dorothy Hinshaw. *Polar Bears.* Minneapolis: Carolrhoda Books, 2000.

Rosing, Norbert. *The World of the Polar Bear.* Richmond Hill, Ontario: Firefly Books, 2006.

Stirling, Ian. *Polar Bears.* Ann Arbor: University of Michigan Press, 1988.

NATIONAL GEOGRAPHIC magazine articles from December 2000, February 2004, and October 2004.

Web sites

http://www.nationalgeographic.com/kids/creature_feature/0004/polar.html

http://www.animalinfo.org/species/carnivor/ursumari.htm

http://www.panda.org/about_wwf/where_we_work/arctic/polar_bear/index.cfm

http://www.rosing.de

http://www.tundrabuggy.com

http://www.polarbearsinternational.org

http://seaworld.org/infobooks/polar bears/home.html

Places to visit
Polar Bears International has Arctic camps for kids to learn about polar bears and visit their habitat.
For information, see: www.polarbears international.org/adventure-learning-program/

INDEX

RESEARCH & PHOTOGRAPHIC NOTES

What makes a successful wildlife photographer? Some people say the photo equipment. Others say good luck or knowledge of your subject. All are right. But I learned that in the vast Arctic wilderness where the polar bear lives, the key to success is a responsible Inuit guide.

I remember arriving on a remote island in the northern Hudson Bay. My guide, Luke Eetuk, came over and introduced himself. He said: "Don't worry about anything but your photography. I will guide you. I will cook. I will set up the tent. Your job is to create photographs. Your images will tell the people outside the Arctic what our home is all about."

For more than three weeks, Luke kept his word. I never was hungry, cold, or afraid. This is important because a tired body with a hungry stomach doesn't do a good job. Being relaxed, even in difficult situations, is very important for a photographer. Under these ideal circumstances, I feel free to move around, look for different angles, wait for low light, and change lenses as often as I need to.

I photograph with 35mm professional cameras, and I prefer film. My lenses range from 16mm fish-eye lenses to 800mm telephoto lenses. To hold the camera steady, I use tripods of varying sizes and, during aerial photography, I use gyrostabilizers.

In the field, there are some challenges that no one can protect you from. In the summer, scores of mosquitoes, black flies, and horse flies, and the inability to take a shower can make life very uncomfortable. In the winter, we grapple with extremely cold temperatures, brisk winds, and 18 hours a day of total darkness.

Why am I doing all this? For the one-of-a-kind experiences! I see animal families acting like us: playing, fighting, having fun, and taking care of each other. I see weather conditions not many people have seen and the aurora borealis lighting up the Arctic during a winter night. Being outdoors is a learning experience. The most important lesson: learning to respect the lives of other creatures.

—NORBERT ROSING

Acknowledgments:
I could not have shot these images without the help of my Inuit friends in Nunavut, Canada; Inuit guides Pakak Qamaniq and Adam Qanatsiaq; Cree guides Morris and Mike Spence; the people of Churchill, Manitoba, Canada; and the polar bear researchers Nick Lunn and Ian Stirling. Special thanks to my wife Elli for letting me go when I needed to and to Robert Buchanan of Polar Bears International for his friendship and support.

The publisher gratefully acknowledges the assistance of Christine Kiel, K-3 Curriculum and Reading Consultant.

Book design by David M. Seager
The body text of the book is set in ITC Century. The display text is set in Knockout and Party Noid.

Published by the
National Geographic Society

John M. Fahey, Jr., *President and Chief Executive Officer*

Gilbert M. Grosvenor, *Chairman of the Board*

Nina D. Hoffman, *Executive Vice President, President, Book Publishing Group*

Staff for This Book

Nancy Laties Feresten, *Vice President, Editor-in-Chief of Children's Books*

Bea Jackson, *Design and Illustrations Director, Children's Books*

Jennifer Emmett, *Project Editor*

David M. Seager, *Art Director*

Lori Epstein, *Illustrations Editor*

Jocelyn G. Lindsay, *Researcher*

Jean Cantu, *Illustrations Specialist*

Carl Mehler, *Director of Maps*

Rebecca Baines, *Editorial Assistant*

R. Gary Colbert, *Production Director*

Lewis R. Bassford, *Production Manager*

Vincent P. Ryan, Maryclare Tracy, Nicole Elliott
    Manufacturing Managers

Cover: Playful and powerful, polar bears have surprisingly expressive faces. *Back Cover:* A polar bear romps with a new toy. *Page One:* A polar bear cub follows his mother. *Title Page:* Face to face with a polar bear.

Library of Congress
Cataloging-in-Publication Data

Rosing, Norbert.
  Face to face with polar bears / by Norbert Rosing with Elizabeth Carney.
     p. cm. -- (Face to face)
  Includes bibliographical references and index.
  ISBN 978-1-4263-0139-1 (trade : alk. paper) -- ISBN 978-1-4263-0140-7 (library : alk. paper)
  1. Polar bear. I. Carney, Elizabeth, 1981- II. Title.
QL737.C27R69 2007
599.786--dc22

2006032847

Printed in China